STEFAN GOLASZEWSKI

Stefan Golaszewski co-wrote and performed in *Cowards* on Radio 4 (2007, 2008) and BBC4 (2009). He produced and performed his first two plays at the Pleasance Courtyard (2008) and the Traverse Theatre (2009) in Edinburgh, and then together as *The Stefan Golaszewski Plays* at the Bush Theatre in London (2009–10). His play *Sex with a Stranger* was first performed at the Trafalgar Studios in 2012. He was the writer, creator and executive producer of BBC3's *Him & Her* (2010–13), winning the BAFTA for Best Situation Comedy in 2014.

Other Titles in this Series

Stefan Golaszewski

SEX WITH A STRANGER

NICK HERN BOOKS

London

www.nickhernbooks.co.uk

A Nick Hern Book

Sex with a Stranger first published in 2012 by Nick Hern Books Limited, The Glasshouse, 49a Goldhawk Road, London W12 8QP

Reprinted with a new cover and revisions to the text in 2014

Cover photo: Jaime Winstone and Russell Tovey in the original production of *Sex with a Stranger* (2012), photograph by Pete Le May

Designed and typeset by Nick Hern Books, London
Printed in the UK by Mimeo Ltd, Huntingdon, Cambridgeshire PE29 6XX

A CIP catalogue record for this book is available from the British Library

ISBN 978 1 84842 255 1

Sex with a Stranger was first performed at Trafalgar Studios, London, on 1 February 2012, with the following cast:

ADAM	Russell Tovey
GRACE	Jaime Winstone
RUTH	Naomi Sheldon

Director	Phillip Breen
Designer	Holly Pigott
Lighting Designer	Emma Chapman
Sound Designer	Andrea J Cox
Producer	The Invisible Dot Ltd

6

Characters

ADAM

GRACE

RUTH

The characters are all in their twenties.

The text incorporates revisions made to the play by the author since its original production, and should be considered the definitive version.

ACT ONE

ADAM *wears trendy blue jeans, a 'going-out' shirt and gel in his hair. GRACE is dressed scantily for clubbing. Whenever she's outdoors she has a man's (ADAM's) jumper draped over her shoulders. She has a bag.*

ADAM *and* GRACE *stand at a bus stop.* ADAM*'s drinking a bottle of Lucozade.* GRACE *is on the phone. She looks at* ADAM, *awaiting an answer.*

ADAM. Adam.

GRACE (*into the phone*). Adam.

She bursts out laughing, eyeing him.

ADAM (*pretending to be interested and amused, laughing*). What? What?!

GRACE (*to* ADAM, *cheekily*). Never you mind. (*Into the phone.*) What's that?

She gives a big laugh. ADAM *laughs too.*

No, he's all right. He's nice. I got a bit upset in the club and – (*Bursts out laughing.*) Abi!

Blackout.

Both sit. She's on her phone. ADAM *laughs when she does.*

GRACE (*into the phone, shocked, laughing*). No… (*Listens, shocked, laughing.*) No…!

She listens, shocked. He offers her the Lucozade. She waves it away.

(*Into the phone.*) And why was that? (*Listens, then shocked, laughing.*) No…! (*Bursts out laughing, then listens for a longer time.*) Yeah and you were right because – (*Listens.*) Oh. Right. Yeah. Definitely.

Blackout.

She's stood on the phone.

GRACE (*into the phone*). No. You go. I'd better go too if I'm honest. He'll probably run away if I carry on like this any longer!

ADAM (*falsely jovial, more to 'Abi'*). No I won't!

GRACE (*into the phone*). Did you hear that?

GRACE *bursts out laughing.* ADAM *laughs.*

(*Into the phone.*) You're so funny. God. (*Listens.*) Okay. Let me know you got home okay, yeah? Sorry you – Sorry. All right. Bye. Bye, babe. Bye.

(*She hangs up, laughing demonstrably.*) She's so funny!

ADAM *laughs too.*

My sister. Abi. There's three of us. Me, Kate and Abi. I'm the middle one. They're so funny.

He laughs.

She's such a character. She's the youngest.

ADAM. They do say that about the youngest.

GRACE. Yeah. They do don't they. Tut. Funny isn't it?

ADAM (*laughs*). Really funny.

GRACE (*putting her phone away*). Mad.

Blackout.

GRACE *inspects the bus timetable*.

ADAM. How long?

GRACE. Twelve minutes.

ADAM. Cool.

GRACE. It's every twelve minutes, so it's not gonna be longer than that.

ADAM. Cool. And how long is it on the bus?

GRACE. Half an hour.

ADAM. Wicked.

She sits. A beat.

GRACE. Someone's tried to smash the glass on that.

ADAM. On what sorry?

GRACE. The timetable.

ADAM. Have they?

GRACE. Yeah.

ADAM. God… Why would you do that?

GRACE. I know…

A beat.

Are you cold?

ADAM. I'm good.

GRACE. Good. (*Yawns.*) Excuse me!

ADAM. Ha!

She laughs. He laughs.

GRACE. Mad isn't it? Such a great night.

ADAM. Yeah. Really cool. Great club.

GRACE. Great club. I've never been there before.

ADAM. Me neither. It's good though isn't it.

GRACE. Really good. Yeah. Great DJs.

ADAM. Awesome DJs.

A beat.

So where exactly is it you live?

GRACE. D'you know Homebase?

ADAM. I don't know the area.

GRACE. I'm about five minutes from Homebase.

ADAM. Oh. Brilliant. Wow.

GRACE. Yeah. Just a five-, ten-minute walk from there.

ADAM. Amazing.

GRACE. Yeah.

A beat.

ADAM. That must be handy. When you need stuff from Homebase.

GRACE. Yeah. It is actually.

A beat.

Blackout.

They stand looking into the distance.

ADAM. Such an amazing club.

GRACE. God yeah. Rob is so funny. Was it Rob? The black man?

ADAM. Robert. Yes. It's his birthday. It was Wednesday but he's celebrating it tonight.

GRACE. Yeah. I've done that. Was that his girlfriend?

ADAM. Katie. Yeah.

GRACE. Oh. Same as my sister. Except she's a Kate. (*Chuckling to herself.*) She's such a Kate…!

ADAM (*chuckles*). Yeah! I don't think it'll last though.

GRACE. What?

ADAM. Robert and Katie.

GRACE. Oh. Right. I thought you were talking about Kate!

ADAM. Who's that?

GRACE. My sister Kate and her boyfriend Jake.

ADAM. No!

GRACE. God!

ADAM. Right. No. I mean I don't think Robert and Katie will last.

GRACE. He's taking her to Rome! He's so gonna ask her to marry him and you're sitting there saying it won't last and I was like –

ADAM. No! Robert and Katie won't last.

GRACE. – I was like, Jesus! Adam!

ADAM (*laughs*). No no no no no. I was saying I don't think Robert and Katie will last. Sorry. I don't think Robert and Katie are that good for each other, actually.

GRACE. Really?

ADAM. Yeah.

GRACE. I don't know. They seemed good together.

ADAM. Yeah?

GRACE. Well I don't know but to an outsider they seemed good together.

He scratches his hand.

ADAM. Yeah. I don't know either. But I think Robert's feeling a bit tied down if I'm honest.

GRACE. No…

ADAM. Yeah.

GRACE. No… I don't think so.

ADAM. But life's like that sometimes isn't it.

GRACE. They seem like such great people.

ADAM. No they are. They are.

Silence. He offers her some Lucozade.

GRACE. No. Thanks.

Silence. She starts laughing.

Oh my God you were such an amazing dancer!

ADAM. Was I?

GRACE. Oh my God!

ADAM. In a good way I hope!

GRACE. Yeah as if! (*Laughs.*) You wish! You wish it was in a good way!

They laugh.

ADAM. That is so offensive…

GRACE. No it's not!

ADAM. Amazing! So funny!

They laugh. He drinks and finishes the Lucozade. He scratches his hand.

I must've been bitten.

She feels her pockets.

GRACE (*worried*). My Oyster.

Blackout.

She searches in her bag. She's wild with worry. He's scratching his hand.

ADAM. It'll turn up.

GRACE. I just put a fucking tenner on it.

ADAM. Shall I have a look?

She searches. Silence.

Could you maybe have left it somewhere?

GRACE. For fuck's sakes!

She searches. Silence.

ADAM. I can pay.

She searches. Silence.

I really don't mind paying.

She finds it in her pocket.

GRACE. There it is.

ADAM. Oh good. Thank God for that.

GRACE (*genuinely exasperated*). It's always in the last place you look.

ADAM. So annoying…

GRACE. I'm glad I found that.

It's awkward. She looks into the distance.

(*Ratty.*) Is that ours? I haven't got my glasses.

He looks with her.

ADAM. Yeah. Maybe. What one do we want?

GRACE. N73.

ADAM. No.

GRACE. Okay.

Silence.

(*Back to normal.*) Really glad I found my Oyster card. I put ten pounds on it this evening.

ADAM. Did you?

Blackout.

Really loud, cold, inhuman dance music. They're in a club. They're stood apart from each other, not dancing, stood alone watching other people dancing, unaware of each other.

Blackout.

They're sat on a bus.

ADAM. That's better.

GRACE. Yeah. I don't like standing up.

ADAM. Yeah. I'm like that.

Silence. Hold on this.

I think I've been on this bus before.

GRACE. Have you?

ADAM. Yeah.

GRACE. Cool.

ADAM. Yeah I'm sure I have.

GRACE. I've been on it loads.

Silence. They just sit there, pretending it's not awkward.

ADAM. I do like buses actually.

A beat.

So you're in recruitment, is that right?

GRACE. Yes.

ADAM. God.

GRACE. I'm cool with it.

ADAM. That's good.

GRACE. It can be difficult I guess. But that's kind of a good thing in a way.

ADAM. Meeting lots of new people.

GRACE. Well not that but yeah.

A beat.

What do you do again?

ADAM. I'm in sales.

GRACE. Oh yeah.

ADAM. But I'm gonna move into social media.

GRACE. Yeah. I remember now.

ADAM. I've got this idea for a website –

GRACE. Yes I remember you saying.

Hold on them just sat there on the bus, looking separately.

ADAM. Busy tonight…

GRACE. Yeah.

Silence. He looks at her.

ADAM. I like your hair.

GRACE. Do you?

ADAM. Yeah.

GRACE. It's my GHDs.

ADAM. Cool.

A beat.

And d'you get it cut like that? Or do you do it all with the GHDs?

GRACE. Erm. Bit of both really. I get it cut. But I get it for half price because my sister used to work there. Abi. She used to be an assistant. And I sort of saw the owner for a bit.

ADAM. Cool.

Silence. Hold on them just sat there on the bus, looking separately.

It was a good club actually wasn't it?

GRACE. It was a good club, yes.

Blackout.

The street. She's bent over, fiddling with her foot. He's just stood there, watching her. Hold on this for a beat, then –

ADAM. You could take them off.

GRACE. I'm fine.

ADAM. The stuff you women have to go through. It's madness.

No response. He watches her fiddling, not knowing what to do. Eventually she straightens up. She's now fiddling with her top, covering herself up, wrapping the jumper round her more. As she does so –

Where's your place?

GRACE. It's about a twenty-minute walk that way.

ADAM. Oh. Cool.

A beat.

I really need a wee.

GRACE. There's a park you can do it in.

ADAM. Oh good.

GRACE. It's nice actually. It's got a pond.

ADAM. Oh cool.

She finishes fidgeting.

Come here…

GRACE. One second.

A second of fidgeting. Then she does. They hold each other.

ADAM. What a night!

GRACE. Yes! What a night…!

They laugh.

ADAM. And this seems like a cool area.

GRACE. Yeah. It is nice actually.

ADAM. Very nice.

GRACE. Yeah. There's lots of amenities. Lots to do. Quite a young crowd but there's also your oldies as well.

ADAM. You cold?

GRACE. No.

ADAM. Good.

He starts touching her face.

GRACE. Yeah. It's not bad actually. You've got your supermarkets, your local shops, there's a Homebase, there's a club, the park. There's a Kebabish down the road. Are you hungry?

He kisses her. Hold on this. He gets more into it than she does. He pulls back.

ADAM (*quiet, so the audience can only just about hear it*). Maybe we should go to the park together. What d'you think?

A beat as they look at each other. She kisses him. He pulls back.

Grace. What d'you think?

She kisses him. It's cold, lustless and this time it goes on for ages. He holds the back of her head. It goes on and on till it becomes uncomfortable for the audience. It doesn't crescendo – just the same kissing, still and stationary, apart from at one point he puts his hand tentatively on her bottom, where it remains, groping her in a way that looks perhaps painful for her. Finally they part and wipe their mouths.

Blackout.

The kebab shop. They sit, eating.

ADAM. Is that nice?

GRACE. It's amazing.

ADAM. This is delicious.

They eat in silence.

I'm starving. I had a shit lunch.

GRACE. What did I have for lunch? Cheese sandwich.

ADAM. Lovely. What cheese d'you put in it?

GRACE. Cheddar.

ADAM. I love Cheddar. I like Brie as well.

GRACE. Yeah.

They eat in silence. Hold on this. Then –

ADAM. D'you want a drink?

GRACE. I'm fine.

ADAM. Coke? Diet Coke?

GRACE. No. It's got caffeine in it. It keeps me awake.

ADAM. Yeah.

GRACE. I won't sleep tonight.

ADAM. Okay.

They eat in silence.

GRACE. Such a great night…

She laughs. He smiles.

Was it you that likes the Harry Potter films?

ADAM. Erm. No. I don't think so.

A beat.

Are they good?

GRACE. I don't know. I guess they must be.

He smiles. They eat in silence.

This is absolutely amazing!

ADAM. Mmmmm!!

They eat in silence. Eventually –

So – Grace – you don't eat any meat?

GRACE. No.

ADAM. Mad… No animal products? No animal products at all?

GRACE. None.

ADAM. Wow. Impressive.

GRACE. I don't know about that.

ADAM. Debbie – the pregnant one tonight –

GRACE. Oh yeah.

ADAM. She goes out with my mate Dave –

GRACE. 'Dave and Debbie'!

ADAM. Oh yeah!

GRACE laughs. ADAM laughs.

GRACE. Sorry! Carry on.

ADAM. She's a vegetarian – Debbie is – and she doesn't eat meat but she does eat fish. You ever done that?

GRACE. No. I've heard of people who do that but I'm not like that.

She wipes her mouth with a tissue. A beat, then –

ADAM. And do you miss meat?

GRACE. Bacon sandwiches.

ADAM. Yes!

GRACE. Oh my God I so miss bacon sandwiches! Sometimes if my flatmate's making one, I'll have a bite on his.

ADAM. Bacon's not bad anyway is it.

GRACE. Yeah.

Silence. They eat.

ADAM. This is yummy.

GRACE. Mmmmmmm!

He watches her eating for a moment. Then, getting up –

ADAM. I'm gonna get a Coke. Sure I can't get you a Coke?

GRACE. Yeah. I don't want to be up all night.

ADAM. Well you can share mine if you fancy it.

GRACE. I'm fine.

ADAM. Cool.

He goes to the counter at the back of the stage. She eats with her back to him. Silence. He stands there with his back to us and her. Hold on this. He looks back at her without her knowing. A beat of his disappointed, despairing, blank look. He looks forward again, his back to her and us. A beat.

Blackout.

Empty stage apart from a shirt that's the same as the one ADAM's been wearing throughout the play, still in its packet from the shop, unopened. ADAM comes on topless. He picks up the shirt, opens it and puts it on. It's creased from being folded in its packet.

ADAM (*calling offstage*). It's creased!

No response. He tuts and harrumphs. He looks at himself in an invisible mirror. He tuts.

What am I gonna do?

He looks in the mirror. No response. He takes it off.

Ruth, it's really creased!

He goes offstage.

(*Offstage*.) Ruth!

Blackout.

They're in the cab. The car radio plays in the front. She's leaning forward, speaking to the invisible cabbie.

GRACE. It's just past Homebase.

She sits back with ADAM.

I love cabs. It makes me feel like I'm famous.

ADAM. I think you'll be famous one day.

GRACE (*pleased*). Do you?

ADAM. Yeah. Of course.

GRACE. I don't know…

ADAM. Of course you will.

GRACE. Tut. I dunno.

A beat.

I wouldn't want to be too famous.

ADAM. No.

Long silence, just sat there looking out of their windows, the radio playing in the front.

GRACE. Such a crazy night.

ADAM. Yeah.

A beat.

GRACE. I had a real chilled day – really nice – just sitting round and vegging out – spoke to my mum, which was nice –

ADAM. Oh. Nice.

GRACE. Yeah.

ADAM. She okay?

GRACE. Yeah.

ADAM. Good.

GRACE. Just a really chilled day. Nice to have a bit of downtime isn't it.

ADAM. Definitely.

Long silence. Car radio. They just sit there. He scratches his hand. He offers her some chewing gum.

GRACE. Thanks.

She takes one and sits there chewing. Silence. Car radio.

And so cool. Getting a cab.

ADAM. Yes!

GRACE. I usually walk!

ADAM. Do you?

GRACE. Yeah. God… This is the life! Jesus… Hilarious…

He smiles for her. Long silence. Car radio in the front. She looks at him and feels the bottom of his shirt.

This is nice.

ADAM. Thanks.

GRACE. Where d'you get it?

ADAM. Can't remember.

GRACE. It's nice.

ADAM. Thanks.

A beat.

GRACE (*about the cabbie*). We should make out. Give him something to look at.

She laughs. He laughs for her. They just sit there, looking out of separate windows, chewing.

Blackout.

Outside GRACE*'s front door.* GRACE *is trying to find her keys in her bag.*

ADAM. It's a lovely house.

GRACE. It's from the sixties.

ADAM. Very nice.

GRACE. Sorry – they're definitely in here.

ADAM. It's fine.

She looks. He's trying to be patient. He points.

They're nice.

GRACE. The lady upstairs does them.

ADAM. Oh. Nice.

GRACE. She's a bit of a bitch but she's cool. (*Signalling around them.*) She looks after the garden as well.

ADAM. Nice.

A beat.

They're not in your pocket are they?

GRACE (*not checking*). No.

She looks in her bag. As she does so –

I'll just have to go in first and check my bedroom's cool.

ADAM. Cool.

She looks for her keys. We can sense his despair.

So who mows the grass? Does the lady upstairs do that as well?

She ignores him. She looks in her bag. She then stops and looks up at him.

GRACE. Have you got condoms?

ADAM. Yeah.

GRACE. I've run out.

ADAM. I've got three.

GRACE. Cool.

She looks in her bag.

Blackout.

Empty stage. A beat. A young woman, RUTH, *walks from stage left across the stage carrying an iron in silence. She exits stage right.*

Blackout.

The club. Music so loud they have to shout above it. We can just about hear them. They can just about hear each other. Big smiles from them both throughout.

ADAM. Come outside!

GRACE (*giggling*). What?!

ADAM. Come outside!

GRACE. What for?!

ADAM. Come outside with me!

GRACE (*giggling*). Why?!

ADAM. I've got something I wanna show you!

GRACE. What?!

ADAM. Just come outside and you'll see!

GRACE. What?!

ADAM. I've got something I want to show you!

Blackout.

GRACE*'s flat.* GRACE *and* ADAM *are hushedly, hysterically laughing, bent double, trying not to make any noise. They shush each other, which only makes them laugh more. They laugh and laugh and shush and shush.*

Blackout.

GRACE*'s flat. The hallway. They're still hysterical, giggling but having to hush themselves. They speak in whispers through their laughter.*

ADAM. Are you gonna tell him?

GRACE. I don't know! I might have to...

ADAM. Grace!

She laughs even more.

Blackout.

GRACE*'s flat again. They're still laughing and whispering through the hysterics.*

ADAM. You should've told me it was there!

GRACE. I didn't expect you to –

ADAM. Shsh!

GRACE. I didn't expect you to tread on it!

ADAM (*loud*). It was a mistake!

She shushes him. They laugh again.

Don't you shush me!

He grabs her.

Blackout.

Outside the club. Music comes from inside the club. He snogs her cold, hard, up against a wall.

Blackout.

Silence and empty stage.

RUTH *comes on with an ironing board. She unfolds its legs, having trouble making them remain up – she doesn't quite know how the thing works. She leaves again, returns with the iron and plugs it in, allowing it to heat up. She then leaves to get* ADAM's *creased shirt, places the creased shirt on an ironing board and irons it in silence. She irons it perfectly, carefully and completely. It's ironed in real time, as long as it takes. The only sound is the sound of the iron. She lifts the shirt and looks at it, finished.*

Blackout.

GRACE's *kitchen. A CD plays quietly.*

GRACE. Shall we have a drink?

ADAM. Erm. I don't know. Are you having one?

GRACE. I don't mind. D'you want one?

ADAM. Yeah. If you do. (*At something by her.*) That's nice.

GRACE. Yeah.

ADAM. For your keys?

GRACE. Yeah.

ADAM. Yeah. Good idea.

GRACE. Yeah.

A beat.

So what d'you fancy?

ADAM. What have you got?

GRACE. God… Lots of things. Pretty much everything I think.
Most of it's my flatmate's but he won't know. What d'you
think?

ADAM. I don't mind. I'll have whatever you're having.

GRACE. Something alcoholic? Non-alcoholic?

ADAM. Erm… Alcoholic? I don't mind really.

GRACE. Okay. God. Look at it all. We could stay up all night
drinking couldn't we?

ADAM. Yeah…!

She laughs. He laughs along.

GRACE. Couldn't we though!

ADAM. Yeah!

GRACE. I'd love to do that. Have you ever done that?

ADAM. Yeah. Once or twice.

GRACE (*with an edge*). Who with?

ADAM (*the tiniest hesitation*). Friends.

GRACE. Oh my God. Abi's done that. Funny… So funny.
God… I can't wait to tell her…!

ADAM. Yes!

A beat.

GRACE. So what d'you fancy?

ADAM. Erm –

Blackout.

They both have non-matching shot glasses she's poured tequila in.

ADAM. That was funny at the door wasn't it?

GRACE. Yeah. Amazing. God.

ADAM. Amazing!

GRACE. D'you want salt and lime?

ADAM. Erm. Yeah. Okay. Sounds good.

GRACE. I've definitely got salt. I don't know if he's got –

ADAM. Don't worry.

GRACE. Actually, he keeps a lot of stuff in his bedroom –

ADAM. Honestly, I'm fine.

GRACE. Okay. Cool. (*About the glasses.*) I didn't know we had these.

ADAM. Ha!

A beat.

(*At the fridge.*) Who's that?

GRACE. My nan. She's dead now.

ADAM. Oh. Sorry.

GRACE. Thanks.

They look at their drinks.

ADAM. Shall we?

GRACE. Yes!

Blackout.

ADAM *waits outside the bathroom.* GRACE *washes her hands and her teeth and uses mouthwash.*

Hold on this for a while – they do the things they would. His phone rings. He's startled and silences it. He watches it flashing in silence.

She flushes and comes out, just as he puts his phone away. She sees. He knows she's seen. She pretends she hasn't.

GRACE. All right?

ADAM. Yeah. Yeah.

Blackout.

GRACE*'s hallway. They don't hold each other.*

ADAM. Such a long hallway.

GRACE. Yes. It is isn't it. I've often thought that.

ADAM. Very clean though.

GRACE. Thanks. We've got a cleaner. She's so fucking expensive.

ADAM. Is she?

GRACE. Yeah.

A beat.

(*At a wall.*) That's my flatmate. I think he worked in France for a bit. He's night manager in the big Sainsbury's.

ADAM. So is he at work?

GRACE. I don't know.

ADAM. Can we find out?

GRACE. I dunno.

A beat.

I met him on the internet. He seems nice though.

ADAM. That's nice.

A beat.

GRACE. Can you guess which bedroom's mine?

ADAM (*immediately*). That one?

GRACE. Yeah.

She giggles.

Well here we are!

ADAM. Yes!

GRACE. I'll just check if –

ADAM. Yeah. Cool.

GRACE. Cool.

Blackout.

ADAM *waits on his own. His phone buzzes and he takes it out of his pocket and watches it flash in silence. He holds it and lets it ring off. He puts it in his pocket. He waits.*

Blackout.

GRACE *comes back on.*

GRACE. All done!

ADAM. Great.

GRACE. The bed's quite low so be careful of your shins.

ADAM. Yeah. Thanks.

GRACE. And I've found you a towel for the morning.

ADAM. Great.

GRACE. D'you have any plans for tomorrow?

ADAM. Oh. You know. Don't know.

GRACE. Cool. Take it as it comes.

ADAM. Yeah.

GRACE. Cool.

She pecks him on the lips. A beat.

ADAM (*through a smile*). So shall I come in? Or are we gonna stand here all night?

GRACE (*through a smile*). Yeah.

Blackout.

ADAM*'s sat in a concert hall, programme in hand, listening to a violin solo.*

Blackout.

GRACE*'s wedding day. She speaks through a microphone. The responses are pre-recorded and sound as if at a wedding – in a big tent, loads of people rustling, laughing, etc. She reads her speech from a piece of paper.*

GRACE. It is no secret that I have always believed in love at first sight. I didn't know if I would but I always held out hope that I'd meet the man of my dreams and fall head over heels in love. (*Clears her throat.*) As a lot of you will know, I kissed many a frog before I found my Prince Charming. But when I met Paul I knew that it was worth the wait. Not only is he a very successful and intelligent man, and a true Christian, but he has also has a great sense of humour and we have an amazing time together. (*Looks up to the audience.*) He is the night sky that lets my star shine. (*Turning to him, reading again.*) Paul, I want to tell you that – I want to tell you that my heart will always be yours. May our hearts live on for the rest of our days – and beyond – intertwined and warm with the glow of our everlasting love. I will always be by your side.

The crowd 'aaaaaah's.

I would like to propose a toast – so if everyone (*Very slightly garbled.*) would be upstanding and charge their glasses –

The sound of everyone standing up.

To my love, my companion and my husband, Paul.

EVERYONE (*voice-over*). To Paul!

Blackout.

GRACE*'s bedroom.* ADAM *and* GRACE *snog, cold, hard. He goes to take her top off. It's difficult. She's letting him but not making it easy for him. Eventually she pulls back.*

GRACE. Sorry. D'you mind if we turn the light off?

ADAM. No. No.

Going to do so –

GRACE (*as if she's being funny*). Thanks. Sorry. I'm a bit of a light-phobic when it comes to these night-time… things…

ADAM. Or we could have the lamp on?

She stops.

GRACE. Erm… Okay. (*Laughs.*) Yeah. Why not?

She turns the light off. The stage is in darkness. She crosses the room in darkness –

(*Walking into something.*) Ow. Fuck.

– and turns the lamp on. The room is dimly lit now. GRACE *is rubbing her shin.*

ADAM. Is that okay?

GRACE. You don't want to turn it off?

ADAM. Erm. I don't know. I don't want to hurt my shin as well!

GRACE. It hurts.

She rubs it. Awkward. Still smirking, he goes over to her.

ADAM. Come here…

He kisses her briefly.

It doesn't hurt.

They kiss, cold. He goes to remove her top again. Again she lets him but doesn't help him. He manages to remove it. Her bra is dowdy, basic, unsexy. She pulls back.

GRACE (*as if it's funny*). Sorry. I don't want to go on like an idiot but I don't feel comfortable with it so I'm gonna put the light on in the hallway and then we can turn the lamp off and the lights will still come in under the door. So it's the best of both worlds and everybody has their fair share. Okay?

Nothing. He just kisses her breasts and tries unsuccessfully to undo her bra.

Adam.

ADAM (*not aggressively, quietly as he kisses her breasts*). Stop going on about the light and help me get your fucking bra off.

A beat. Ambiguity in GRACE*'s response.*

Blackout. Silence.

End of Act One.

ACT TWO

RUTH *and* ADAM's *living room.* RUTH *comes in with two cups of tea.* ADAM *sits onstage, in clothes different from (looser, less impressive than) those in the first act. He no longer has gel in his hair. He coughs over her first line.*

RUTH. Chloe showed me her wedding dress.

ADAM. Sorry. I couldn't hear you.

RUTH. Chloe showed me her wedding dress.

ADAM. Oh God.

She hands him the mug.

RUTH. Careful. It's hot. No it was nice actually.

ADAM (*taking the mug*). Thanks.

RUTH. It's white.

ADAM. Like she should be wearing a white dress!

RUTH. Yeah! And it's one of those ones that covers her boobs –

ADAM. She hasn't got any.

RUTH (*laughing*). Adam!

She spills a bit of tea.

Shit.

Blackout.

He's still on the couch. She's on her hands and knees, scrubbing where she spilt the tea. He drinks from a cup of tea. Hers sits on the floor.

RUTH. So it's like it covers them so it looks like she's got them but we don't have to see them – as if we could! – and there's these big roses on it –

ADAM. Oh no…

RUTH. Yeah. I mean it's quite nice – for her – but –

ADAM. It's so typical.

RUTH. Oh yeah.

ADAM. And fucking roses…

RUTH. Yeah. She's always liked roses. Unfortunately. And she's having this garland – she showed me the designs on the internet – like a garland for her hair with roses in it.

ADAM. What is it with roses?

RUTH. Yeah. I know! Weird. It's pretty though. It'll look pretty on her –

ADAM. But –

RUTH. – but – yes – stop with the roses, Chloe!

She laughs.

ADAM. What is wrong with her?!

RUTH. I know…

ADAM. All this fuss!

RUTH. I know…

ADAM. It's just a wedding!

She laughs for him. A beat. As she finishes scrubbing –

RUTH. It's okay though because we're going to be wearing these lemon dresses – they're a bit like my maxi dress – the one with the animals on it – but they're lemon – and they won't have any roses on them so I think it won't be too bad at all really.

Silence. She sits next to him.

What time are you going out?

ADAM. I'm meeting them at seven.

She looks at her phone and puts it down again.

Blackout.

Empty stage.

ADAM (*offstage right*). What shall we have for lunch?

A beat. RUTH *comes on from stage left and crosses the stage to stage right.*

RUTH. Did you call me?

ADAM (*offstage*). What shall we have for lunch?

RUTH. Erm. I don't know. We've got ham.

ADAM (*offstage*). Yeah.

RUTH. And there's bread.

He doesn't respond.

We could use some of my cheese slices and do toasted sandwiches.

ADAM (*offstage*). What about a salad?

RUTH. Yep.

ADAM (*offstage*). We could get lettuce and stuff.

RUTH. Shall we talk about it when you're finished?

ADAM (*offstage*). Someone was saying if you avoid mixing carbs and proteins you lose weight quicker.

RUTH. Who was saying that?

ADAM (*offstage*). I dunno.

RUTH. You don't need to lose weight.

No response.

Well it's always good to be healthy.

No response.

I mean, I could probably do with shedding a few pounds myself.

No response.

My trousers were really tight this morning.

No response.

Yeah. Chloe goes to the gym at lunchtimes.

A beat as she waits for a reply.

Blackout.

They're looking round a supermarket. She has a shopping basket with just salad cream in it. He holds a bag of chopped leaves.

RUTH. Or an iceberg?

ADAM. It's Italian. And it's already chopped. Save you chopping it.

RUTH. Yeah.

He puts it in their basket. They browse.

ADAM. What else d'you put in a salad?

RUTH. Avocado?

They browse. Silence.

Dressing?

ADAM (*negative*). Mm.

RUTH. Are you all right?

ADAM. Yeah. I'm fine.

RUTH. Is there anything I can do?

ADAM. No I'm fine.

They browse in silence.

RUTH. Oo. Yeah. I might get a can of Coke.

ADAM. It's full of sugar.

RUTH. I don't like Diet, do I.

ADAM. Coke Zero?

RUTH. Yeah.

She doesn't get one. They browse in silence.

I saw a man the other day who looked like Robert.

Cucumber?

Blackout.

In the queue for the till.

RUTH (*whispering*). 'Six items' means six items. That's so annoying though isn't it. Look at her. It just holds everyone up. It's really selfish though isn't it?

ADAM. Yeah.

A beat.

RUTH. If it said 'baskets only' I'd understand. But look at her. It's disgusting. What does she think she looks like?

ADAM. Mm.

A beat.

RUTH. It says 'six items only'. I can't believe she's even being served. D'you know what I mean? I can't believe they're serving her. It's ridiculous.

Silence. They queue.

ADAM. Maybe the peppers count as one.

Silence. They queue.

Blackout.

*The streets. They're walking with groceries. They both have a
bag in each hand. On the first line,* ADAM *stops* RUTH *at a
crossing from being run over. She smiles a thank you to him.*

RUTH. I said what you said to say about Dan Fisher.

ADAM. Oh good.

RUTH. I said it in the group meeting while he was on reception
– and I was cool and I didn't get annoyed – I just said it like
you said to say it.

ADAM. Good.

RUTH. Yeah. It was actually.

*She goes to speak and a police siren approaches, passes,
then departs. It's too noisy to speak so they stand in silence,
her looking to him and smiling. He smiles thinly back. When
it's passed, she speaks on. They remain stood still.*

I mean I was talking to Soph about it at orchestra and she
said I should've left it but –

ADAM. You had to do something about it.

RUTH. No. Thank you.

ADAM. He wouldn't have done it if you'd been a man...

RUTH. Well...

*They move across the road. She puts one of her bags into her
other hand.*

(*Referring to his bag.*) If you put that in that one, we can
hold hands.

A beat. He does so.

Blackout.

RUTH *and* ADAM*'s living room. He's sat on the sofa, texting. She's offstage.*

ADAM. Yeah. Definitely.

RUTH (*offstage*). Because if we put the speakers on the walls with the wall brackets, we can get some plants or something by the telly. Or another option I thought of – well Candice – Have I told you about Candice? She's the nice new lady that cleans our ward. She was talking about it's what her brother's got and I thought it sounded like something we could do – and it's just a thought so just say if you don't like it – what I thought is if we could put the telly on the wall with the wall brackets and then that opens up all that space for us to do something else with it. Get a new set of bookshelves. Put some of my books up.

ADAM. Yeah.

RUTH (*offstage*). What d'you think?

ADAM. Yeah. Definitely.

A beat.

(*Looking up from his text.*) Could we put the salad leaves underneath? So it's like a bed?

A beat.

Ruth.

RUTH (*offstage*). I'm doing it.

A beat.

But d'you think that's a good idea? The wall brackets. I mean, it's not like I'm trying to hog all the space for my books. But a bookshelf's for life. It's a good investment. The bookshelves in my parents' house they got as a wedding present. And they still use them.

ADAM. No. I know. It's a great idea.

She pokes her head in. He stops texting and looks up as if he wasn't texting.

RUTH. Seriously. I'm not. I know we don't need them so if you don't like it it's fine.

ADAM. No. It's fine.

RUTH. I'll pay for them myself.

ADAM. It's fine.

RUTH. Cool. Who are you texting?

ADAM. I'm on the internet.

RUTH. Cool.

She smiles, lingers for a beat and leaves. He sends the text and puts his phone to the side.

(*Offstage.*) Because you can put your books there too if you like. It's just nice having books around isn't it? They're nice to look at. And then we'll have these bookshelves for ever. We can take them with us.

ADAM. Could we cut the ham into strips?

RUTH (*offstage*). Okay.

ADAM. Thanks.

RUTH *comes onstage with scissors.*

RUTH. Sorry for going on about the bookshelves.

ADAM. Don't worry.

RUTH (*as if it's funny*). I'm such a loser. No wonder you want to go out tonight!

They both laugh. Hold on this.

Blackout.

Pub. RUTH *and* ADAM *are sat onstage. Her friends and his friends are talking (invisibly and inaudibly). They don't speak. Music from four years ago plays.*

Eventually, ADAM *leans over to her. They both speak above the noise around them.*

ADAM. What do you do?

RUTH. English.

ADAM. Oh. Cool. (*About himself.*) Geography.

RUTH. Oh. Nice.

ADAM. Yeah. It is nice. Yeah.

    A beat.

    I'm Adam, by the way.

RUTH. Ruth.

ADAM. Ruth. How d'you know Chloe?

RUTH. We lived on the same corridor.

    ADAM *nods, interested.*

    How about you?

ADAM. Amnesty. Yeah. Amnesty. She's great. She's really turned the group around.

RUTH. Well that's Chloe!

    They laugh. Silence. They look at other conversations. She tries to think of something to say.

    So Geography…

ADAM. Yes.

RUTH. Is that the political side? Or the geographical? Or –

ADAM. Well we touch on them all but I'm actually more focused on the environmental.

RUTH. Oh. Wow. And what's that like?

ADAM. It's actually quite frightening.

RUTH. I bet it is. Yeah.

ADAM. Some of the things they reckon's going to happen.

RUTH. Tut. I bet…

A beat.

ADAM. It's nice here isn't it?

RUTH. Yeah. It's a really cool place.

Blackout.

RUTH *and* ADAM'*s living room. They're eating their lunch on the sofa.*

ADAM. This is lovely. Thank you.

RUTH. No. Thank you. It was your idea.

They eat.

So what is it you're doing tonight?

He puts a load of food in his mouth. He waits to chew it all, indicating his mouth is the reason he isn't answering. She smiles at it. Eventually he swallows and answers.

ADAM. What's that?

RUTH. What are you guys up to tonight?

ADAM. Oh. Just the normal, probably.

He puts more food in his mouth.

RUTH. That'll be nice.

ADAM (*with his mouth full*). Yeah.

They eat. Silence.

RUTH. We should've got some peppers or something. Spice it all up a bit.

ADAM. It's fine.

They eat. Silence.

RUTH. So is it just down The Prince?

He gets up. During the following, he goes over and puts a CD on.

ADAM. It's Robert's birthday isn't it? You know what he's like.

RUTH. He's such a twat.

ADAM. Yeah. I know. But he's a mate.

RUTH. Well he's never very nice to you.

ADAM. Yes he is. And he had a big one last year didn't he. Which I think that's why he wanted to do a big one again this year. I think it's hitting twenty-six.

RUTH. Really?

ADAM. Yeah.

RUTH. That's weird.

ADAM. No it's not.

Music from four years ago starts and plays beneath the following. He returns to his seat and eats. She eats.

He's got a new job. Did I tell you?

RUTH. Yeah. It's great.

ADAM. Yeah.

They eat. Music.

RUTH. Are you gonna have to go clubbing again?

ADAM. One minute.

He leaves the stage. A beat. She doesn't eat. He returns with the bottle of salad cream.

What was that?

RUTH. Are they gonna make you go clubbing?

ADAM. Erm. Maybe. I dunno. You know what he's like.

RUTH. God…

ADAM. I know… I know… Maybe I'll just come home early…

He squirts salad cream over his food. She squirts it into a puddle at the side of her plate.

But then, I guess, it is his birthday…

RUTH. You could get him to go somewhere else.

ADAM. Yeah. But it's his birthday though isn't it? You know what he's like.

RUTH. How d'you mean?

ADAM. He's just annoying isn't he.

RUTH. Yeah. I bet you wish you could just stay in and watch *Mad Men.*

ADAM. Yeah…

They eat.

But if it's his birthday, I kind of have to go don't I? It's like – on my birthday – what if he'd made us go clubbing. It's like him phoning us and insisting we went clubbing. After you'd booked the lane and everything. It's the same.

RUTH. Maybe.

ADAM. I don't want to go but if he wants me to go I can't really back out of it now. It's kind of rude.

RUTH. I don't know…

A beat.

ADAM (*at her plate*). Are you gonna finish that?

RUTH. Yeah.

Blackout.

RUTH *and* ADAM*'s bedroom.* ADAM *stands in just a towel, wet. He holds a hanger with a pair of blue jeans (the ones we've seen him wearing throughout Act One) hung on it, fresh from a shop, the tags still on.*

ADAM. Is it okay to wear these?

He waits. He waits. He waits. RUTH *comes in, drying her hands on a tea towel.*

That smells nice.

RUTH. Thanks.

ADAM. What d'you think about these?

RUTH (*hides her surprise*). When did you get them?

ADAM. Erm. Dunno. Thursday? What d'you think?

RUTH. They're nice. Yeah. Very nice.

ADAM. Yeah?

RUTH. Yeah.

ADAM. There was a mannequin had them on.

RUTH. What you wearing them with?

ADAM. I bought this.

He takes out the shirt he was wearing in Act One. She hides her surprise.

RUTH. That's really cool. I'll just turn the oven down.

RUTH *leaves.* ADAM *stands there in silence. He dries himself as he waits.*

(*Calling from offstage.*) Maybe…

Silence.

ADAM. What?

RUTH (*offstage*). Maybe if you –

Silence.

ADAM. Maybe if I what?

RUTH (*offstage*). One minute.

A brief silence then she comes on.

What about one of your T-shirts? You look nice in them.

ADAM. I'm not gonna wear a T-shirt in a club.

RUTH. So you are going clubbing?

ADAM. I dunno.

RUTH. It's not like you're trying to impress anyone.

ADAM. No of course not.

RUTH (*trying to be funny*). Who are you gonna impress with your dancing?!

ADAM. Why are you being like this?

RUTH. Why am I being like what?

ADAM. Like this.

RUTH. It was a joke.

ADAM. It wasn't funny.

RUTH. Okay.

A beat. They both look at the shirt and jeans.

ADAM. How's the pie?

RUTH. Yeah. It's nice.

Blackout.

A restaurant. ADAM *and* RUTH *look through menus on the sofa.*

ADAM. Have you seen some of the adjectives they use? Have a look at the starters.

RUTH *smiles and looks back through the menu.*

Number five.

She turns a page back and finds it and laughs.

RUTH. 'Infused'!

ADAM *laughs.*

ADAM. Amazing isn't it?

RUTH. And look at number eight. 'Marinated'!

ADAM. I always think that in restaurants. They have the oddest things. There was this Chinese – or it was more of a Cantonese I suppose – it was near where I did some work experience last summer – I was at the Centre for Climate-Change Research –

RUTH. Oh!

ADAM. Yeah. And they had this menu with –

He's interrupted by a waiter.

Erm. Yes. I think so. Are you ready?

RUTH. Yes.

ADAM. Okay. To start, can we get the garlic bread to share – the one with mozzarella on it – thanks – and… olives? D'you like olives?

RUTH. Yeah!

ADAM. And some olives please. Again, to share. (*To* RUTH.) For mains?

RUTH. Thank you. (*Studying the menu unnecessarily.*) Can I have the Calabrese please?

ADAM. That doesn't have capers in it does it? Good. And I'll have the Sloppy Giuseppe.

They share a tiny smile.

And a glass of the Merlot – Large. Is Merlot okay?

RUTH. Yes. Lovely.

ADAM. And a bottle of Peroni. And can we get some chilli oil with the pizzas? Thanks. Yes that's all. (*To* RUTH.) I think?

RUTH (*with a chuckle*). That's enough for me.

ADAM (*to the waiter*). How long will our table be? Okay. Thank you.

The waiter goes away.

I booked well in advance.

RUTH. I really don't mind.

She tries to lighten the mood.

'Sloppy Giuseppe'…!

They both laugh a little.

How do they come up with these things?

They both laugh a bit more.

ADAM. There's probably a chef in Italy called Giuseppe who's really messy and he just made such a mess of a pizza and it tasted amazing and they named it after him!

RUTH. Yes!

They both laugh. They drink. The laugh settles. A beat.

I'm glad you like olives.

ADAM (*a noise of agreement*). Mm!

RUTH. I love olives.

ADAM. Mmm. Me too. I had these really lovely black olives once – my uncle works in the catering industry –

RUTH. Oo. You lucky bastard.

ADAM*'s slightly taken aback by this and tries not to be. He laughs, finding her genuinely fresh and surprising. She laughs too.*

Sorry!

ADAM. No! No! I am a lucky wotsit. We get a fresh turkey at Christmas.

RUTH. Oo. Lovely.

ADAM. And anyway he got these olives – straight from Italy – little shrivelled black ones. Very delicate texture.

RUTH. Oo. Lovely. They sound lovely.

ADAM. They really were.

RUTH. Do you prefer them stuffed or unstuffed?

ADAM. Oo. I don't know.

RUTH. I like the green ones stuffed with feta.

ADAM. Yes! I love those ones!

RUTH. I could eat about a million of them.

ADAM. I do like them stuffed, actually. You're right. But you've got to make sure it's feta in there and not just some cheap cheese.

RUTH. Yeah. My mum gets them at the deli in Sainsbury's.

ADAM. Oh. Lovely.

RUTH. Yeah. She got a big pot of them for my dad at Christmas.

ADAM. That's really nice. Wow! She sounds like a great mum!

RUTH. She is.

A beat.

ADAM. But just to finish my anecdote –

RUTH. Yes! Of course. Sorry! Blabbering on!

ADAM. He got us these olives and they were just completely moreish. So moreish. Really delicious.

RUTH. Mmm. Lovely.

ADAM. Yeah.

A beat of silence.

I'm sure these olives will be delicious as well.

RUTH. Yes! Definitely.

ADAM. If they ever do their jobs and get us a bloody table!

RUTH. Ha!

A long silence, awkward on the sofas.

So what do your parents do for a living?

Blackout.

RUTH *and* ADAM*'s flat.*

ADAM (*shouting*). I wasn't fucking looking at her!

RUTH (*sitting with her feet on the sofa*). Now who's swearing?!

ADAM. Take your shoes off.

She tuts and moves her feet off the sofa.

(*Calmer.*) Okay. Listen to me. Ruth. Stop being a fucking idiot and just listen to me –

RUTH (*starting to cry*). Adam!

ADAM. – and listen to what I'm saying. I looked in her direction. I'm not saying that in the course of the entire evening I didn't look once in her direction. Of course I fucking did! You don't expect me to just ignore our friend for the entire fucking evening just in case you decide I'm looking at her! That's rude! You want me to be rude to our friends now?

RUTH. I want you to not stare at her –

ADAM (*exploding again*). I wasn't staring, you fucking prick!

RUTH (*exploding too, crying*). To not stare at her when you're supposed to fancy me!

ADAM. Of course I fancy you!

RUTH. Oh yeah! It's wild!

ADAM. Shut up!

RUTH. It's wild! You're always ripping my clothes off!

ADAM (*turning on her*). You shut your fat fucking mouth!

Blackout.

Pub. She cries silently in her hands. His anger is barely containable. He speaks quietly. He has a mouthful of beer left in his pint glass.

ADAM. Stop. Crying.

She cries silently in her hands.

Stop. Fucking. Crying. People are looking.

She cries silently in her hands.

Finish that and we'll go. This is fucking ridiculous.

She cries silently in her hands. He finishes his pint.

It's not my fault you can't handle your fucking drink.

Blackout.

RUTH *and* ADAM's *living room. They watch a DVD. Hold on this. TV audio plays* – Mad Men, *Series Three.*

RUTH. So are you going for a drink first?

ADAM (*annoyed*). Ruth...

He pauses it. TV audio stops.

What?

RUTH. Are you going for a drink? Before the club?

ADAM. Yeah. I think so.

RUTH. Cool. That'll be nice.

A beat.

Where you gonna go?

ADAM. I don't know.

He goes to un-pause the DVD and she interrupts.

RUTH. Because if you're somewhere local maybe I should –

ADAM. It'll be in town.

RUTH. Okay.

ADAM. Sorry.

RUTH. No.

He smiles and un-pauses it. TV audio.

I just thought it might be nice of me to say happy birthday to Robert.

ADAM. Well you've got your concert tomorrow haven't you.

RUTH. Yeah.

He gestures for her to watch the TV. They do. She snuggles up to him. They sit there watching it. She kisses his cheek. He just looks straight ahead. Hold on this, the sound of the TV the only sound, her hand on his chest.

Blackout.

GRACE *sits on stage in pyjamas, wearing her glasses. She's just straightened her hair with her GHDs. Her make-up is on. Inspirational, light, happy, contemporary music plays that she doesn't react to in any way as she turns her hair into the style it was in Act One. When this is done, she removes her glasses and checks herself, close to the mirror.*

Blackout.

RUTH *and* ADAM's *bathroom.* ADAM *puts deodorant on, his jeans on but shirtless.* RUTH *appears with the perfectly ironed shirt.*

ADAM. Thank you.

RUTH. That's okay.

ADAM. Sorry if I sounded angry.

RUTH. No. You didn't.

ADAM. You know what I'm like when I'm late.

RUTH. Don't worry. I know.

She smiles. He smiles.

You smell nice.

ADAM. Thanks. Yeah. It's Lynx. Africa.

RUTH. Lovely. When did you get that?

ADAM. Erm. Dunno. During the week?

RUTH. You should've said. I'd've got that instead of the Nivea.

ADAM. It's all right.

A beat. She removes a label from the back of the jeans.

Thanks.

He goes to put his shirt on.

RUTH. Are you gonna shave?

He stops putting his shirt on.

ADAM. I wasn't going to.

RUTH. Okay. Cool.

ADAM. I thought I'd give myself a night off.

A beat as she looks at him.

What?

RUTH. I dunno. I quite like it when you shave –

ADAM. It's not permanent.

RUTH. No I know.

ADAM. I just can't be bothered.

RUTH. I just like it how it normally is. That's all. But I also like it like that so it's cool.

A beat.

Well anyway. It's good to have a change isn't it?

ADAM. Yeah.

RUTH. I might put some highlights in my hair.

No response. He puts the shirt on, doing up the buttons in silence. She watches him. When they're all done up –

ADAM (*scratching his hand*). What d'you think?

RUTH. It's a nice fit.

ADAM. D'you think?

RUTH. Yeah. It's lovely. (*With no gap.*) Who else is gonna be there?

ADAM. What d'you mean?

RUTH. Who else is gonna be there?

ADAM. Tonight?

RUTH. Yeah.

ADAM. Oo. I don't know. Erm. Me, Robert, probably Robert's brothers, erm – (*Quickly.*) John, Dave, Mike and Alex – (*Normally.*) I guess some of the twats from the council. Dunno.

RUTH. That'll be nice.

ADAM. Yeah.

RUTH. Very nice.

A beat.

And what's Katie doing tonight?

ADAM. I dunno.

RUTH. Weird. You'd think she'd go out for her boyfriend's birthday.

ADAM. Yeah. It's a lads' thing though isn't it.

RUTH. They're such a weird couple.

ADAM. I know…

RUTH. What about Debbie? I hope Dave's not dragging her out clubbing in her condition.

ADAM. Of course he won't. She won't be there. It's a lads' thing.

RUTH. So none of the girls are going?

ADAM (*a big laugh*). Well I can't promise you we won't go to a pub with women in it!

RUTH. No but I don't mean that do I. I know they're a weird couple but it just seems really weird Robert wouldn't invite Katie and her lot.

He starts to leave.

ADAM. I think they did a thing on Wednesday.

RUTH. It just seems weird though doesn't it.

ADAM (*offstage*). It's not weird.

RUTH. Well it is a bit weird.

He pokes his head onstage –

ADAM. It's not weird.

– and leaves again.

RUTH. Imagine if you didn't invite me out for your birthday. Everyone would think it was weird.

ADAM (*offstage*). It's not his birthday. (*Coming back on with the jumper* GRACE *was wearing earlier*.) His birthday was on Wednesday.

Blackout.

ADAM *sits on the sofa putting his shoes on.* RUTH *sits beside him in silence, watching. He puts one shoe on and ties the laces. Then –*

ADAM. Have you got any chewing gum?

RUTH. Yeah. In my bag.

ADAM. The brown one?

RUTH. Yeah.

He puts the other shoe on and ties the laces. She sits there in silence, watching.

Blackout.

RUTH *and* ADAM*'s living room.* RUTH *stands there.* ADAM*'s offstage.*

RUTH. I'm gonna be so nervous tonight. God... I'll just be sitting here thinking of my solo all night. Because if I muck this up you know he'll never trust me with a solo again. That's what happened to Soph.

ADAM (*offstage*). You'll be fine.

RUTH. I hope so. (*As if it's funny.*) I'll probably drive myself crazy thinking about it. You'll come back later and find me sat here like a gibbering wreck!

ADAM (*offstage*). Don't be silly. Get a good night's sleep tonight and you'll wow them all tomorrow.

RUTH. If I can sleep!

ADAM (*offstage*). Take a Nytol.

RUTH. Yeah.

He comes on. His hair is gelled as in Act One. She's visibly surprised.

ADAM. What?

RUTH (*smiles*). Nice.

ADAM. Thanks.

He starts putting the jumper on, careful of his hair. She considers saying something. She says something else.

RUTH. What sort of time d'you think you'll be back? I don't mean it like that but –

ADAM. I don't know really. Could be late.

RUTH. Will you text me when you're on your way?

ADAM. Yeah. Of course. Don't wait up though. I don't want to disturb your violin sleep.

RUTH (*laughs*). No. Thank you.

He smiles at her and leaves the stage. During the following, we see RUTH *disintegrate.*

ADAM (*offstage*). D'you know what? Thinking about it, I might even just crash at Robert's or something. I'll have to see how it goes. They were talking about everyone crashing at his tonight. Because it'll be late and I don't want to get a night bus because they can be really dangerous can't they and I don't want to disturb you. So actually, thinking about it, we'll probably all just crash at his.

RUTH (*trying to sound normal*). Okay. Cool. Or you could get a cab?

ADAM (*offstage*). Expensive.

He comes back onstage. RUTH*'s face picks up again.*

RUTH. When you've made your millions from your website, you'll be getting cabs everywhere…!

He just smiles at her.

ADAM. Is that okay then? If I crash at Robert's.

RUTH. Yeah. Of course. Do what you want.

ADAM. Have you seen my keys?

She leaves the stage. He puts chewing gum in his mouth. She comes back on with his keys.

Thanks.

A beat – he looks at his phone.

I'd better be off.

RUTH. You'll be back for the concert though won't you?

ADAM. Of course I will! Blimey. As if I'd miss that!

RUTH. I'm so nervous.

ADAM. You'll be fine. You never stop practising that thing.

Blackout.

RUTH *and* ADAM*'s living room.* ADAM*'s ready to go out.*
RUTH *stands there.*

RUTH. Are you sure? You've only had a salad.

ADAM. I'll be fine.

RUTH. Sorry.

ADAM. Don't worry.

RUTH. The pie's looking nice.

ADAM. Honestly.

RUTH. You'll need to line your stomach.

ADAM. I'll be fine.

RUTH. Cool. Cool

She watches him get ready, scratching her hand.

Maybe tomorrow, after the concert, we should go to bed
early. Get an early night.

ADAM. Sounds good.

RUTH. Take our time over it.

ADAM. Yeah. Cool.

A beat.

I'd better go.

RUTH. They're not gonna go to any strip clubs are they?

ADAM *laughs. Seeing this,* RUTH *laughs too.*

ADAM. What?! Where did that come from?! No! You know us!
As if we'd go to some seedy little strip club!

RUTH. Sorry – I had to ask or I'd be sitting here going mad thinking of you looking at women like that and you all laughing.

ADAM. Of course I won't be looking at women like that! Of course we won't go to a strip club.

RUTH. Okay. Sorry. I just thought there must be a reason Katie's not going and –

ADAM. Ruth.

RUTH (*as if it's funny*). – I had this image of like these wild women and you boys all going mad about them.

ADAM (*laughs*). I've got to go. I'll see you tomorrow, yeah?

RUTH. Yeah. Cool. Sorry. (*As if it's a shared joke*.) Make sure you text me and let me know how the dreaded clubbing goes!

ADAM. Definitely! But we won't go clubbing. I'm sure.

RUTH. Really?

ADAM. I dunno. But yeah. I'll text you. Of course. Let you know how awful it is!

RUTH. Yeah! And make sure you text me any Robert and Katie news…!

ADAM. Definitely! Yes!

RUTH. They're such a funny couple!

ADAM. Yes!

　　A beat.

　　Right. I'd better be off.

　　He moves off.

RUTH. Cool.

　　A beat.

　　I think I'll have a tidy. Clean the bathroom. Your study could do with a clear-out.

ADAM (*turning back, like a bullet*). I wouldn't bother.

RUTH. When did you last clean it?

ADAM. Seriously. Everything's in an order, I know where everything is. I like it like that.

RUTH. I'll just give it a once-over. Sort out your folders.

ADAM. Honestly. Leave it. Relax. Have some time to yourself. Don't worry about it. Read your book.

RUTH. I don't mind.

ADAM. Seriously. Read your book. I don't want you sorting out my folders on a Saturday night!

They laugh.

Seriously. Have some downtime. Read your book. Get in the right frame of mind for tomorrow.

RUTH. Okay.

ADAM. Good. Well I'll see you tomorrow. I'll see you afterwards, okay? Good luck.

RUTH. Thanks.

ADAM. I'll be in the foyer.

RUTH. I might be a bit longer than normal because they'll want to go through how it went and the solo and everything.

ADAM. Cool. No worries. I'll wait.

RUTH. Cool. Thanks.

ADAM. And no tidying!

RUTH. No. Okay. Thanks.

ADAM. Bye then.

RUTH. Bye.

She goes in for a kiss. They kiss, a peck on the lips. He leaves.

RUTH *stands onstage alone, dead still.*

She leaves the stage. Pause on the empty stage. She returns with her book and a piece of her steaming-hot apple pie. She sits on the sofa and removes her shoes. She gets her phone out and puts it beside her, in her line of vision.

She reads her book. She eats her pie, blowing on it because it's hot. She reads her book. Hold on this for a long time. She then looks up for a moment with a thought. She then returns to her book. Hold on this.

Blackout.

The End.